Flavors
from the
Void

Recipes inspired by nothing.

Introduction

This book is a collection of varied recipes from various chefs in the Pacific Northwest. There is no uniting genre of food or culinary style. There is no focus on a specific ingredient, a specific course, or a specific restaurant. There is, in fact, only one real uniting element in the dishes that follow: Nothing.

We run Float On, a float tank center based in Portland, Oregon. If you've never heard of float tanks, flip to the last pages of this book and we'll fill you in on all the salty details. For those of you already familiar with our strange line of work, you may be curious as to how culinary inspiration can come out of an environment whose goal is to provide the least amount of sensory input possible.

Since opening in 2010, we've run programs for athletes, poets, dancers, writers, and more. The largest in scale have been our Art Program (which spawned a 150 piece artbook), our Music Program (which produced almost 30 tracks composed inside our float tanks), and now our Chef Program (which has culminated in this very book).

We launched this, the most delicious of our undertakings, in 2012, by offering Portland chefs four free floats over the course of a month. During this time, they dreamed up, refined, and prepared dishes based on their own experiences in the tank. The end result is a series of recipes, simple and advanced, savory and sweet, that are unique in their development. They were created to appeal to the taste buds of someone just getting out of a float, when the senses are fresh and awakened. As you might imagine, they are exceedingly tasty no matter what your mental state.

Bon appétit!
Ashkahn, Antonio, Josh, Graham, and the rest of the Float On crew

Contents

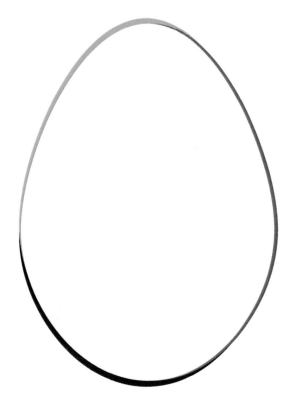

Appetizers

Black Hash — 2

Tomato Soup with a Twist (GF) (V) — 6

Green Fruit Salad (V) — 8

Chilled Quinoa Salad (GF) (V) — 12

Float Salad (V) — 14

Mjadra and Caramelized Onions (GF) (V) — 18

Lebanese Nachos (GF) (V) — 22

Black Hash

Charles Grey O'Neill

My goal for this recipe was to create an image of a float in a bowl. The yolk represents you and is surrounded by darkness. When you cut into it, the yolk flows over the black and the plate components become one.

I decided to use tongue in the hash because like a sensory deprivation tank, it's not something a lot of people are accustomed to.

Some may be hesitant to try it, but the methods I used to prepare the tongue is pleasing to the palate. It imitates a classic breakfast dish, but in a new way. Both a float and this dish are about being able to embrace the darkness and new things.

Ingredients

Recipe serves four people

¾ liters of water

½ cup of salt

¼ cup of sugar

1½ teaspoons of T.C.M.
  curing salt

1 bay leaf

3 garlic cloves

½ teaspoon of black pepper

½ teaspoon of mustard seed

½ teaspoon of coriander

½ teaspoon of dill seed

¼ teaspoon of allspice

⅕ thyme bunch

5 cow tongues

4 purple potatoes

3 tablespoons of butter

3 thyme sprigs

2 tablespoons of hay ash

8 eggs

fleur de sel

Purple Oxalis for garnish

salt and pepper

Directions

1. Combine water, salt, T.C.M., bay leaf, garlic clove, black pepper, coriander, dill seed, all other spices, and the thyme bunch in a medium pot over high heat. Bring to a low boil. Remove from heat and cool over ice bath. Bag with tongue and brine for 12 days. Cook sous vide at 158° F for 48 hours.

2. Cool and remove from bags. Discard brine. Peel off outer skin of the tongue and dice into small pieces. Parboil purple potatoes, then peel and dice to the same size as the tongue.

3. Melt butter in a pan over medium heat. Add thyme and minced garlic and sauté for one minute. Add potatoes and cook for two minutes. Add tongue and cook for three minutes. Add hay ash until desired color is accomplished. Season with salt and pepper to taste.

4. Cook eggs sunny-side-up and cut with 3.5 inch ring cutter.

5. Place in a dark bowl with hash on bottom, each serving topped with an egg sprinkled with fleur de sel and garnished with Purple Oxalis.

Tomato Soup with a Twist

Robert "Bama" Pugh

This soup is inspired by my post-float sensations. About five minutes after I get out of a float tank, I have a feeling that is only heightened by sitting with a warm cup of tea.

So thinking outside the box, I took a classic tomato soup and added a hint of honey and lemon flavor. The result is one of the best soups I have ever made, and it is always in demand.

Ingredients

Recipe serves eight people

4 medium red onions *diced small*

6 medium carrots *diced small*

8 ribs of medium celery *diced small*

½ pound of butter

4 cups of white wine

2 quarts of vegetable stock

12 large tomatoes *quartered*

5 roma tomatoes *quartered*

16 ounces of clover honey

½ cup of Cajun seasoning

½ cup of parsley

½ cup of cilantro

4 tablespoons of paprika

4 tablespoons of minced garlic

2 cups of basil

2 large lemons

12 ounces of goat cheese

sea salt and pepper *freshly cracked*

Directions

1. In a large stockpot, melt butter. Add onions, carrots, and celery. Sweat, then deglaze with white wine.

2. Add chicken stock, all tomatoes, honey, parsley, paprika, garlic, basil, Cajun seasoning, and salt and pepper to taste.

3. Simmer for 45 minutes to one hour.

4. Use blender to combine ingredients, straining out large chunks.

5. Squeeze in fresh lemon juice to taste.

6. Garnish with goat cheese and top with basil.

Green Fruit Salad

Kerri Sullivan

After my floats, I realized all I wanted to eat were greens and fruits.

I wanted very much the energy accompanied by greens, but without the hearty, savory norm it usually brings forth in flavor.

I decided to make a fruit salad and puree. That would suit to be the foundation of this experiment because I would blend finely chopped spinach
into a puree.

A mango puree is the perfect way to disguise greens in a sweeter dish!

So voilà, thus I give you this recipe and all its glorious flavors!

Enjoy!

Ingredients

Recipe serves six to eight people

2 mangoes

1 nectarine

1 Bosc pear

1 Honeycrisp apple
or apple of your liking

1 blood orange

1 Valencia orange

1 banana

10 strawberries

½ bunch of spinach

2 tablespoons of dried goji berries

1 medium piece of ginger
chopped

½ cup of lemon juice

2 teaspoon of cinnamon

1 quart of yogurt

Directions

1 In a pot, add 2 cups of water and chopped pieces of ginger. Let this simmer while preparing the rest of the dish (approximately 20 to 30 minutes).

2 Then into a small bowl, pour ginger water over dried goji berries. Let sit for 5 minutes. Strain and set aside until the last step.

3 In another bowl pour in the ½ cup of lemon juice with a ½ cup of water.

4 Chop the apple into bite-sized pieces. Let this soak in the lemon water and set aside.

5 Finely chop the ½ bunch of spinach. Put this into a bowl and set aside.

6 With a blender or similar kitchen device (i.e. immersion blender), puree both of the mangoes and the nectarine together. Pour the puree into a bowl of spinach and mix with a quart of yogurt and 2 teaspoons of cinnamon.

7 Mix all together, cover, and set aside to chill in the refrigerator.

8 Lastly, into a big bowl, chop into bite-sized pieces the pear, oranges, strawberries, and banana. Strain the apple pieces and add them to the fruit bowl. Combine the yogurt and mango puree into the mixture.

9 Mix the ingredients together. Top with the ginger-soaked goji berries.

10 Chill or enjoy immediately!

Chilled Quinoa Salad

Sean McGlohon & Samantha Ellis

After a long float full of relaxation, Samantha finds herself being super hungry.

"I am always in such a place of bliss that I cannot fathom cooking a meal. I knew the perfect dish must be prepared in advance, but able to keep well for a few hours in the fridge and still taste delicious after leaving the tank."

This meal has a perfect balance between sweet and savory and is both filling and refreshing after a float!

Samantha Ellis is a wellness instructor, photographer and chef. Her business is Squid and Cat – squidandcat.com

Ingredients

Recipe serves two to three people

1 cup of quinoa

2 cups of water

¼ teaspoon of salt

½ stalk of celery *diced*

1 medium cucumber *diced*

3 green onions *chopped*

⅓ sweet onion
  Walla Walla or Vidalia, diced

½ cup of cranberries

2 tablespoons of freshly squeezed lime juice *or to taste*

1 tablespoon of olive oil

salt and pepper to taste

Directions

1. Rinse and drain quinoa under cold water before placing in a medium saucepan along with 2 cups of water and ¼ teaspoon of salt.

2. Over medium heat, bring to a boil and let cook for 5 minutes.

3. Reduce heat to low and simmer for 15 minutes, or until water has been absorbed.

4. Remove from heat and fluff with fork. Set aside to cool to room temperature. Add celery, green onion, sweet onion, cranberries, and cucumber. Toss to combine.

5. Add lime juice, olive oil, salt and pepper to taste, tossing together to combine.

6. Serve chilled, or at room temperature if desired.

Float Salad

Jeffrey MacKay

This recipe was truly inspired by my floating sessions. I began with all kinds of ideas, and on my second float I just let this vision come to me. I would say that about 80% of the final version just popped into my head while I was floating.

My inspiration was to create something that I had never made before and that was inspired by the floating process. I knew I wanted it to be creative, healthy, and colorful. The original vision that had come to me was a spicy version of this concept, but it turned into this as the final product. I hope that you will enjoy eating it as much as I enjoyed creating it.

Description

Juiced spinach, celery, and cucumber in a chia seed broth; carrot creme fraiche 'slaw with chopped mint; shaved almonds, yellow raisins, apple, and ginger in hazelnut oil on top of sliced beets and alfalfa-clover sprouts, with a dried banana chip to top it all off!

A juicer is needed to create this recipe.

Ingredients

Recipe makes three individual salads

3 spinach handfuls *that will fit into the juicer*

1 celery stick

¼ large cucumber *peeled*

1 tablespoon of chia seeds

1 large carrot *peeled*

1 teaspoon of creme fraiche *to taste, but less is more*

4 chopped mint leaves

3-4 teaspoons of shaved almonds

3-4 teaspoons of yellow raisins

½ apple

1 teaspoon of ginger

2 tablespoons of hazelnut oil

1 large beet *cut in quarters*

alfalfa-clover sprouts *small handful*

3 dried banana chip

Salt and pepper can be added to taste

Directions

1   Start by grating the carrot, apple, and ginger into a bowl. Add olive oil, cream fraiche, salt/pepper, mint, almonds, and raisins.

2   Let it chill in the refrigerator. For optimal flavor, let it chill for a few hours.

3   Juice the spinach, celery, and cucumber to form your "float" broth. Add chia seeds and set aside.

4   Cut the beet and arrange in the bottom of your bowl. Pour in enough broth to cover the bottom of your bowl to create a "floating" effect. Add sprouts on top of the beets.

5   Give your carrot coleslaw a final mix and scoop about a tablespoon on top of the sprouts. Sprinkle with a few extra chia seeds and garnish with a banana chip.

Mjadra and Caramelized Onions

Izzeldin Bukhari

I come from Palestine where we have the Dead Sea, which is naturally loaded with so much salt that you float on it easily. We call it the *dead sea* because nothing can thrive in that water.

This location is one of the most valued healing spots in the country. A lot of people use it for these benefits.

I am glad to see wonderful people doing this concept world-wide to help others. After a float, I feel how my body is recharged and relaxed, my mental state clear and my appetite ready for delicious, warming food full of vitamins and minerals.

Lentils contain high levels of protein and are a great source of iron. They also prevent digestive disorders, with rice added for more fibers, and spices and caramelized leek to complement the flavors.

Izzeldin Bukhari is a chef with a focus on Middle Eastern cuisine – saahha.com

Ingredients

Recipe serves four people

1 cup of brown lentils *sorted for debris and soaked for 30 minutes*

3 teaspoons of extra-virgin olive oil

2 garlic cloves *minced*

1 teaspoon of turmeric

½ teaspoon of cracked black peppercorn

1 medium leek *thinly sliced*

½ onion *cut into small cubes*

1 teaspoon of kosher salt or to taste

1 cup of jasmine rice

½ teaspoon of ground cumin

½ teaspoon of ground coriander

½ teaspoon of cayenne pepper

2½ cups of vegetable stock or water

1 squeeze of fresh lemon juice

optional – Greek yogurt for serving

Directions

1   Preheat stockpot over medium heat. Sauté the ½ onion and garlic in the olive oil for a minute, then add the rice and spices and mix well. Let cook for a minute, then add the lentils and mix again.

2   Add water or stock and bring to a boil. When the water boils, cover the stockpot and turn the heat all way to low and let simmer for 20 minutes. In the meantime, take the thinly sliced leek and caramelize it over medium heat until it turns brown and crunchy, but take care not to let it burn.

3   When the thin slices of leek are done caramelizing, scatter on top of the lentils and rice as garnish and serve.

Lebanese Nachos

Linda Dalal Sawaya

One Sunday evening on my way to Float On for the chef's program – with an empty stomach – this recipe floated into my mind.

Earlier that day, a friend had asked where to find the best nachos for happy hour, so nachos were on my mind. Perfect for the chef recipe invitation, but how to create a new variation?

As the author of a well-loved Lebanese cookbook, they had to be Lebanese nachos! The details of the ingredients emerged in random order during my float sessions: sprouted lentils, gluten-free garbanzo flour chips, tahini instead of cheese, spicy garbanzos in lieu of black beans. Voilà!

My creative, float-inspired, healthy, and yummy Middle Eastern take on nachos!

The crackers, tahini, sprouts, and veggies can be prepped ahead and kept on hand for assembly. Enjoy!

Linda Dalal Sawaya is a chef and author
Alice's Kitchen: Traditional Lebanese Cooking

Recipe serves four to six as an appetizer

Gluten Free
Garbanzo-Garlic Chips
make ahead of time

2 cups of garbanzo bean flour

1 cup of oat flour
plus ½ cup for rolling dough

1 cup of ground sesame seeds
grind in a food processor

½ cup of whole sesame seeds
optional, for rolling dough

1 cup of ground golden flax seeds

1 tablespoon of salt

1 teaspoon of black pepper

2 cloves of garlic *mashed into a paste with 1 teaspoon of salt*

2 cups of water

1 tablespoon of baking yeast

1 tablespoon of baking powder

For the list of Toppings see page 26

Requires a food processor

Ingredients and Directions

Gluten Free Garbanzo-Garlic Chips

1 Dissolve yeast in lukewarm water and let it active for 5 minutes.

2 Mix in garlic and salt paste.

3 Mix flours, baking powder, seeds, salt and pepper together well, and gradually mix into the yeast and water until everything is blended. Add additional flour or water and mix well to achieve a dough that doesn't stick to your hands or is too dry.

4 Cover with a cloth and place in a warm spot to rise for an hour.

5 Preheat oven to 375° F.

6 Form a ball using one cup of dough and then flatten it on a baking sheet lined with parchment paper, using flour and/or whole sesame seeds to prevent it from sticking, and roll it into ⅛ inch thickness.

7 Use a pizza or cookie cutter to cut into chip-sized triangles or 3 inch circles. Collect dough trims and roll into a ball to add to remaining dough. Continue until all of the dough is used up.

8 Let rolled-out dough rest for 15 minutes. Bake on lowest oven shelf for about 10 minutes. Move to top oven rack for another 5 to 10 minutes, until they are golden and crisp.

9 Remove from baking tray and cool. Use when completely cool or store in an airtight tin. If the chips have softened, crisp them up in the oven for 5 minutes.

Sautéed Garbanzo beans

1 1 cup of dry garbanzo beans (soaked in water overnight) or 2 cups of canned.

2 2 tablespoons of clarified butter (coconut or olive oil as a vegan option)

3 2 cloves of garlic, mashed with 1 teaspoon of salt

4 Add a dash of cayenne pepper *or to taste*

5 While dough is rising, drain garbanzo beans and cook in 2 cups of water for 10 minutes over medium heat. Drain liquid and set beans aside.

6 Heat 2 tablespoons of clarified butter (or oil) in a sauté pan. Add garlic to the pan along with garbanzo beans. Sauté over medium high heat, stirring frequently for 10 to 15 minutes until beans are golden. Sprinkle with cayenne pepper in the last few minutes of sauté.

7 While beans are cooking and crackers are baking, prepare other toppings and tahini sauce.

Toppings

1 ½ cup of diced cucumber

2 ½ cup of diced tomato

3 ½ cup of shredded red cabbage

4 ½ cup of diced peppers *red, yellow, orange*

5 ½ cup of chopped green onions

6 1 cup of sprouted French lentils or other sprouts such as alfalfa *sprouted ahead of time*

7 ½ avocado *sliced*

8 ¾ cup of tahini sauce
recipe follows from Alice's Kitchen: Traditional Lebanese Cooking

9 ¼ teaspoon of sumac for garnish

Tahini sauce

1 2-3 cloves of garlic *chopped*

2 ½ teaspoon of salt

3 1 cup of tahini *sesame seed puree*

4 ¼ cup of warm water

5 ⅓ to ½ cup of lemon juice

6 2 tablespoon of parsley *finely chopped*

Put all ingredients in a processor bowl and pulse until smooth, adding parsley at the end.

Assembly

1 Place a single layer of chips on a large serving platter. Add a layer of sautéed garbanzo beans, then drizzle with ¼ cup of tahini sauce. Add shredded cabbage, lentil sprouts, diced cucumber, lentil sprouts, green onions, and tomato, drizzling tahini sauce between each layer to hold it all together and to give it flavor.

2 Finish the top with avocado slices and top with the remaining tahini sauce. Sprinkle with sumac to add a colorful, lemony zest.

Enjoy!

Entrées

Wild Mushroom Creamed Kale — 30
Crostini with Poached Egg

Thai Green Curry Ⓥ — 34

Tenderloin Tar Tar Brot — 38

Sicilian Grandma Pizza — 42

Seafood Cakes — 46

Grilled Chicken Arugula Salad — 50

Pla Laam
Bamboo Roasted Trout with Sticky Rice — 52

Blue Cheese and Spinach — 58
Stuffed Pork Loin

Wild Mushroom Creamed Kale Crostini with Poached Egg

Rob Walls

A body in a float tank has a buoyancy and heft that reminded me of a poached egg.

Poached eggs are great because they're basically little sauce dispensers, and egg yolks are one of my favorite sauces.

The kale preparation is based on a dish I had at the now-defunct restaurant Wafu. A hunk of crusty bread soaks up the tasty run-off of the egg yolk and the creamy, garlicky kale.

Throw some bacon and roasted mushrooms in there and you've got a pretty damn lovely meal.

Rob Walls is a chef and the owner of Double Dragon – doubledragonpdx.com

Ingredients

Recipe serves two people

Tools

1 skillet with lid

1 bunch of kale

1 shallot *minced*

2 cloves of garlic *minced*

1 cup of heavy whipping cream

3 strips of bacon

1 tablespoon of white miso

2 tablespoons of Calvados brandy

½ pound of baby Shitake mushrooms

2 eggs

2 slices of thick rustic Ciabatta bread

1 tablespoon of olive oil

1 pinch of crushed red pepper

white pepper *freshly cracked*

salt *to taste*

Directions

1. Preheat oven to 400° F.

2. Dice bacon. Heat a skillet over medium heat and add olive oil, then bacon.

3. Cook until the bacon has a nice color to it, then use a slotted spoon to transfer bacon onto a paper towel. Leave as much olive oil in the skillet as possible.

4. Add shallot and garlic to skillet. Add a pinch of salt. Add crushed red pepper. If it needs more olive oil, feel free to add it.

5. Sweat the shallot and garlic over medium-low heat until translucent.

6. Rinse and chop the kale into thin ribbons.

7. Once the garlic and shallot have reached a nice softness, deglaze the skillet with brandy.

8. Bring it to a simmer and add miso and heavy cream, stirring together. Once stirred together, taste for seasoning. Add more salt if necessary. It should be aggressively seasoned, as this is the flavor your kale will take on.

9. Add in the kale, stirring and bringing all contents to a slow simmer. Cover the skillet with its lid.

10. Now bring some water to boil in a small pot.

11. In a bowl, toss the mushrooms in olive oil, salt, and white pepper. Lay them out on a sheet tray and place in preheated oven. Roast the mushrooms aggressively until they get some nice color to them. Be patient and try to get them as flavorful as possible.

12. Once the water has come to a boil, add some salt to the water. It should taste as salty as the ocean but not as salty as a float tank.

13. If you have small tea cups, grab two of them and crack one egg into each. If the yolk breaks, discard and start over.

14. Now brush your hunks of bread with olive oil and sprinkle with salt. Place in the oven to toast.

15. Once the mushrooms are finished roasting, they can be set aside with the bacon for garnishing.

16 Check in on your kale. Be patient with it as it will take time to soften up. Once it has reached your desired texture, taste for seasoning, adjust as necessary, then cut the heat, cover it with the lid, and leave it be.

Poached Egg

17 Bring your water down to a very gentle simmer. Have a slotted spoon at the ready. Gently drop each egg in the water. The best method is to partially submerge your tea cup, so as to ensure the most gentle entry possible for the eggs. The white of the eggs will begin to stretch out in tendrils in the water. Gingerly use your slotted spoon to coax each egg into a tight oval. Cook the egg to your preferred consistency. As they begin to take some shape, about a minute in, you can gently use the slotted spoon to take them out of the water and carefully poke the yolk to see their texture. Once they've reached your desired consistency, set them aside in a bowl of warm water.

18 Check on your toast. Once it's nice and crunchy, you've got all your elements and you're ready to plate.

19 Use a nice large round plate or shallow bowl for plating.

20 Place the toast in the center. Top with your desired amount of creamed kale. Create a bed in the kale in which the egg can safely lie. Garnish with bacon and mushrooms. If you have a nice pepper flake like togarashi or Korean crushed red pepper, this can dress up the egg a bit, but it's not essential.

Now enjoy!

Thai Green Curry

Jake Farrar

As I was floating, my mind kept drifting back to how I wanted
Thai Green Curry for dinner. So this is what I decided to create.

Jake Farrar was established as a prominent vegan chef based out of Portland.
He will be remembered and celebrated for nurturing his family
and community through his life's work (June, 2015).

Ingredients

Recipe serves four to six people

2 blocks of 16 ounce firm tofu
*excess water pressed out and
cut tofu into bite-sized cubes*

¼ cup of cooking oil
*no flavor, high heat oil, safflower
or sunflower are the healthiest*

2 tablespoons of soy sauce
*use wheat free Tamari if you
want the curry to be gluten free*

1½ cups of yellow onion *¼ inch slices*

6 cups of eggplant *large bite-sized
chunks (Japanese eggplant preferably)*

4 cups of cauliflower *bite-sized florets*

3 cups of red bell pepper
two inch by half inch slices

4 cups of snap peas *snow peas, or
green beans, two inches long*

6 cups of coconut milk *full fat*

8 kaffir lime leaves

1 tablespoon of pure sesame oil

1 cup of green curry paste

1 tablespoon of fresh lime juice

2 teaspoons of sea salt

1 cup of cilantro leaves

1 cup of Thai basil leaves

1 cup of green onions
one inch sliced on bias

*carrot can be used in place of
red bell pepper if desired*

Directions

1 Heat nonstick frying pan over high heat. Add 1 tablespoon of oil and ½ teaspoon of salt per block of tofu.

2 Fry tofu on high heat, flipping cubes as needed until crispy and golden brown on all sides. Depending on the size of your pan, you may need to cook the cubes in batches.

3 Finish with 1 tablespoon of soy sauce per block of tofu, flipping cubes around to coat evenly. Remove from pan and set aside.

4 Heat remaining non-flavored oil (2 tablespoons) in large stockpot.

5 Add onions and eggplant. Cook on medium high heat, stirring occasionally until parts of onions and eggplant start to turn golden brown.

6 Stir in red bell pepper and cook for 1 minute more.

7 Add cauliflower and stir.

8   Add coconut milk, kaffir lime leaves, and salt.

9   Bring coconut milk to simmer, then add snap peas, snow peas, or green beans.

10 Mix well and reduce heat to low. Gently stir in cooked tofu, curry paste, and sesame oil.

11 Once green vegetables are cooked to desired consistency, remove from heat.

12 Lastly, add lime juice and half of the fresh herbs. Mix gently.

13 Use remaining herbs as garnish.

Green Thai Curry is often served with jasmine rice. Substitute brown rice if desired.

Enjoy!

Tenderloin Tar Tar Brot

Micky Thornton

I was really hungry after my first float. Like, really-really hungry. Even with a huge meal, I still felt unsatisfied. Following my first float experience, I wanted to come up with the hardiest, most decadent, rich and savory thing possible.

A tartar brat seemed to fit this concept perfectly. I spent the rest of my floats fantasizing about making it better and more detailed, but mostly I thought about eventually eating it.

Gluttony has always been my biggest motivation for creating food.

Special Thanks to Tom Daley for helping with preparation and development of this dish.

Ingredients

Recipe serves one person

Candied Bacon

1 tablespoon of apple cider vinegar

1 tablespoon of bourbon

1 tablespoon of brown sugar

1 teaspoon of cinnamon

1 teaspoon of cardamom

1 teaspoon of salt and pepper *combined*

2 pounds of bacon
ends and small pieces are fine to use

Tar Tar

1 bread roll *bratwurst bun*

2 pounds of beef tenderloin *minced*

4 quail eggs

1 tablespoon of shallots *minced*

1 tablespoon of gherkin pickles *minced*

1 tablespoon of banana peppers *minced*

1 tablespoon of peppercinis *minced*

1 teaspoon of garlic *minced*

1 tablespoon of stone ground mustard

1 teaspoon of rosemary

1 teaspoon of thyme
freshly minced, very fine

1 teaspoon of lavender, toasted
*5 teaspoons in a tin foil pouch
(with perforated holes) cooked at
300° F, until dry and crumbly*

1 teaspoon of salt and pepper

Candied Bacon Relish

Requires half of the Candied Bacon

¼ cup of sweet pickle relish

2 tablespoons of gherkins pickles *brunoise (a ¹⁄₁₆ inch dice cut)*

2 tablespoons of shallots *brunoise diced*

2 tablespoons of red onions *brunoise*

1 tablespoon of peperoncini's *minced*

1 tablespoon of banana peppers *minced*

1 tablespoon of fresh rosemary

1 teaspoon of balsamic reduction *¾ of a cup to 1 cup of balsamic, simmer until it reduces to a tar, about 10-15 minutes on low heat*

Bacon Salsa

¼ cup of roma or heirloom tomatoes *diced small*

2 tablespoons of shallots *minced*

1 tablespoon of cilantro *minced*

1 tablespoon of red onions *minced*

1 tablespoon of garlic *minced*

1 lime *zested with a cheese grater and juiced*

½ pound of bacon

1 teaspoon of salt and pepper *combined*

Combine bacon salsa ingredients. This will be used in the final steps.

Directions

Juice

1. Mince onions and garlic.
2. Mix with tomatoes, shallots, pulled cilantro. *fresh cilantro stick, pull leaves off*
3. Combine all together.
4. Set aside to marinate until you're done crisping the bacon.

Crisp Bacon

1. Mince raw bacon.
2. Put on medium heat.
3. Render fat (remove bacon from pan once crispy, and save rendered fat).
4. Reserve fat in pan.
5. Using the pan emulsification method, make a dressing using juice from the above recipe, until fully emulsified. *do not refrigerate*
6. Keep bacon at room temperature.
7. Add crispy bacon just before serving.

Tar Tar

1. Trim the beef (reserve fat and silver skin).

2. Robot Coupe (or immersion blend) the reserved trimmings and mix with minced beef, combine with quail egg yolks.

3. Fold mixture gently with all ingredients, making sure it doesn't turn to mush.

4. Roll into *bratwurst shapes* with a plastic wrap.

5. Partially freeze for an hour or two until it is firm on the outside.

6. Unwrap and smoke in a cold smoker for one day before grilling (smoking develops a skin on the outside so it is less fragile).

7. Chill (refrigerate until ready to grill).

Candied Bacon

1. Cut bacon pieces shorter than an inch.

2. Mix all dry ingredients and toss to thoroughly coat raw bacon.

3. After coating bacon, add liquid and toss while assuring a pasty consistency.

4. Place on silpat.

5. Bake at 300° F on a cooking sheet for 25 minutes to render the bacon fat.

6. Finish at 425° F until crisp (8-10 minutes, or pull before bacon becomes burnt).

7. Reserve half for the step below and use the other half combined with the *Candied Bacon Relish. see ingredients*

Putting it all together

1. Shape the bread roll into a *pretzel roll* (spray with water, using brush or hands, then sprinkle lightly with salt).

2. Put in oven to toast at 350° F for 8-10 minutes.

3. Cut open roll, and smear on *Candied Bacon Relish.*

4. Grilled tar tar brot can go into a bread roll, if desired.

5. Spoon on *Bacon Salsa. see ingredients*

6. Between brot and bun put shards of *Candied Bacon.*

7. Place 3 fried quail eggs or 3 raw quail egg yolks on top of the brot.

Enjoy!

Sicilian Grandma Pizza

Matt Kedzie

This pie recipe is inspired by both whole grains and friends.
I would like bakers at home to enjoy the variety of tastes found in different grains.
Much like fruits and vegetables, freshly-milled whole grains have distinct flavors.
Also, I cannot think of a better gathering than one that involves pizza.

Ingredients

Recipe serves four people

Crust

1½ cups of flour *white*

5 cups of flour *Fife, Spelt, Emmer, or similar flour*

1 cup & 2 tablespoons of water at room temperature

1½ teaspoons of salt

¾ teaspoon of active dry yeast

2 tablespoons of olive oil

Toppings

Top the pizza with ingredients you desire (below is a list of suggested items to add)

3 ounces of fresh mozzarella *or 4 ounces shredded mozzarella*

7 ounces of crushed, canned tomatoes

½ ounce of basil

1-2 ounces of sliced meat or veggies

Directions

The flour you choose will have an obvious impact on the result. I prefer organic, USA-grown white flour, which can be found in the bulk section of any well-stocked market. A small amount of whole wheat, spelt, or farro flour will add a pleasant taste, texture, and color to your pie. Look for these in bulk as well, or order online.

Dough

1 Mix dry ingredients in a big bowl, then add water to the dry stuff. Mix with your hands, pinching and squeezing, until the dough comes together as a semi-uniform mass. Add the oil, using more pinching to incorporate. To create the final shape, gently pull the edges of the dough together to a point. Place in an oiled container and let it be for 8 to 13 hours at a cool room temperature. If it's warm, try 6 to 8 hours. As the dough ferments and expands, it will become more flavorful because of the long rest.

2 Gently remove your dough onto a counter, quickly shape it once more, and place on an oiled steel pan. The pan used here is 6 by 10 inches, but similar sizes will work fine. Once more, the dough needs time to build up gas and flavor. 2 to 3 hours at room temperature in the oiled pan is good. Take this time to go for a 90 minute float or take a nap. (You need to relax too after all this recipe reading!) The dough will naturally start to fill the pan. With a light touch, pull the corners of the dough, pressing if necessary, until it reaches the edges of the pan.

Baking

Preheat your oven to 475° F.

This pizza will taste delicious with a crispy, fried bottom. The inside will be airy and light, and the dough will taste of slightly soured wheat.

The bake is done in three steps.

1 First bake the naked, risen dough for 7 to 10 minutes until the top is just set. Remove the hot pan and place it on your stovetop.

2 Top your dough with crushed, canned tomatoes and drizzle with olive oil. Return the sauced pie to the oven until the sauce is lightly cooked, about 4 to 6 minutes. Remove the pie and top it with anything else you desire: mozzarella, meat, veggies, etc...

3 Continue baking until cheese is bubbly and lightly flecked with color, or until the toppings caramelize and the bottom is golden brown.

Let the pie cool before slicing and serving. Top with fresh basil, extra virgin olive oil, and Parmesan.

Seafood Cakes

Sarah Arkwright

After my floating experiences, I would emerge both relaxed and hungry! I didn't want to get weighed down by a heavy meal, but I needed something satisfying. Of course, eggs had to be involved in some way!

I loved the idea of seafood cakes floating on a bed of arugula. The cakes are a bit lighter than some because I add zucchini to the mix and use panko instead of a heavier breading. The egg yolk provides a creamy element that mixes the whole experience together.

Sarah Arkwright is the owner of
The Egg Carton – eggcartonpdx.com

Ingredients

Recipe serves four people

½ pound of cooked crab meat
shredded and checked for shells

½ pound of cooked bay shrimp
(shrimp meat) lightly chopped

½ cup of shredded zucchini *drained*

¼ cup of bread crumbs

1 tablespoon of fresh lemon juice

1 tablespoon of wasabi paste

3 eggs *lightly beaten*

1 teaspoon of salt

½ teaspoon of pepper

neutral oil
vegetable or canola oil for frying

1 cup of panko
Japanese bread crumbs

4 poached eggs
*or eggs cooked your way,
a runny yolk is recommended*

Salad

arugula

aged balsamic vinegar

olive oil

salt or black pepper *freshly cracked*

Directions

1   Combine the crab, shrimp, shredded zucchini, bread crumbs, lemon juice, wasabi paste, salt and pepper in a large bowl by hand, form into 8 equal patties, and set patties onto a baking tray.

2   Place tray in the freezer for 15 to 20 minutes to allow the patties to firm up slightly. *At this point, you can choose to freeze the patties for up to three months wrapped in plastic wrap and sealed in a freezer safe bag.*

3   In a Dutch oven or large pan, heat approximately ¼ to ½ inch of oil (enough to come half way up the seafood cake) to 350° F.

4   Beat the eggs in a shallow bowl and put panko in a separate shallow bowl.

5   Dip the seafood cakes into the egg wash, then into the panko, then into the hot oil.

6   Cook each side until brown: approximately 3 to 4 minutes. Set aside on paper towels.

7   In a medium bowl, drizzle arugula with balsamic vinegar, toss, then drizzle with oil, and toss again. Top with salt/pepper to taste.

8   To assemble, place approximately ½ to 1 cup of arugula per plate and top with 2 seafood cakes. Top with the poached egg and (if desired) a drizzle of balsamic.

This makes a great appetizer too! Just cut the size of the cakes in half as well as the portion of salad. If possible, use medium sized eggs. Serve everything else as normal.

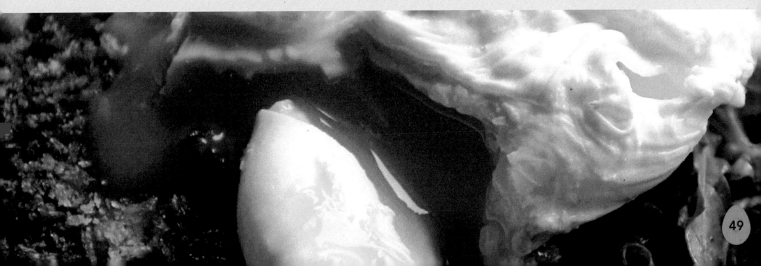

Grilled Chicken Arugula Salad

Daisy Bactad

During my floats, all I could think of were refreshing flavors. Cucumbers came to mind first, then citrus and salads. I thought to myself, 'Why not put them all together?' So I did. The combination made a great, refreshing dish. I hope you enjoy it as much as I do.

Ingredients

Recipe serves two to three people

Blood Orange Vinaigrette

2 ounces of champagne vinegar

4 ounces of olive oil

1 blood orange *zested and juiced*

1 teaspoon of fresh thyme *minced*

1 garlic clove *minced*

1 teaspoon of fresh parsley *minced*

1 teaspoon of fresh chives *minced*

Whisk together vinegar, garlic, herbs, and blood orange. Slowly add oil while whisking. Season with salt and pepper.

Grilled chicken

2 chicken breasts

1 garlic clove

1 teaspoon of fresh thyme

½ teaspoon of red chili flakes

½ of a lime *juiced*

2 tablespoons of olive oil

Salad

1 pound of arugula

¼ cup of hazelnuts *toasted and chopped*

1 red bell pepper

½ English cucumber *sliced*

1 orange *peeled and sliced*

¼ cup of blue cheese *crumbled*

1 red onion *thinly sliced*

Directions

1   Toss all ingredients in a bowl. Marinate chicken breast for 20 minutes. Grill chicken to perfection. Slice chicken into strips.

2   Lightly oil red bell pepper. Roast on high heat until pepper is completely charred on the exterior. Cover pepper with plastic wrap or place inside closed brown paper bag until cool. Peel, seed, and cut into strips.

3   In a bowl, combine chicken, roasted pepper, oranges, and onions. Toss with dressing and place over a bed of arugula. Top with hazelnuts and blue cheese.

Enjoy!

Pla Laam Bamboo Roasted Trout with Sticky Rice

Tanasapamon Rohman "Goy"

Floating allowed me to relax and clear my mind of my daily life. It brought back vivid past memories of friends, family, and the food we enjoyed together in Northern Thailand.

With my current connection with food, I feel that Pla Laam, from my experience, is a very unique and creative dish to share with others.

Tanasapamon Rohman is the owner of Chiang Mai – chiangmaipdx.com

Tools

Large bamboo stalk *16-18 inch long section, open on one end, closed on the opposite end*

Open grill with charcoal

Mortar and pestle

Large tub or sink

Small sauce ramekin or bowl

Steaming tray or rice cooker with steaming option

Large bowl and medium pot

optional – food processor

Ingredients

Recipe serves two people

whole trout 10 ounce to 1 pound *or other medium-sized whole fish*

2 cups of sticky rice

10 large Napa cabbage leaves

1 lemongrass stalk

½ cup of chicken stock

2 ounces of soy sauce

⅛ teaspoon of cumin

⅛ teaspoon of coriander *ground*

1 tablespoon of cilantro *chopped*

¼ teaspoon of white pepper *ground*

2 tablespoons of Thai fish sauce

½ teaspoon of fresh Thai chili *crushed*

7 cloves of garlic *crushed*

3 tablespoons of sugar

4 tablespoons of lime juice

Directions

Preparation time one day

Cooking time 20-30 minutes

Fish marinade

1   Crush 5 cloves of garlic and combine with chopped cilantro and white pepper. Add soy sauce, cumin, and coriander and stir until mixed well.

2   Combine fish and marinade in a large bowl, make sure the bowl is covered, and let sit overnight in the refrigerator for at least 3 hours.

Bamboo preparation

1   Thoroughly scrub and clean the bamboo stalk inside and out.

2   Soak bamboo stalk under cold water in a large tub overnight. Be sure that the bamboo is fully immersed in the water for the full duration.

Sticky rice preparation

Soak 2 cups of sticky rice in water overnight or a minimum of 5 hours.

Cooking fish

1   Remove fish from refrigerator and marinade. Take one stalk of lemongrass and lightly crush it to begin the release of juices. Insert the lemongrass stalk into the fish's mouth and extend it through the cleaned stomach area.

2   Next, wrap the fish in a few napa cabbage leaves, covering both sides of the fish until the skin is no longer exposed. Insert the wrapped fish into the bamboo head first.

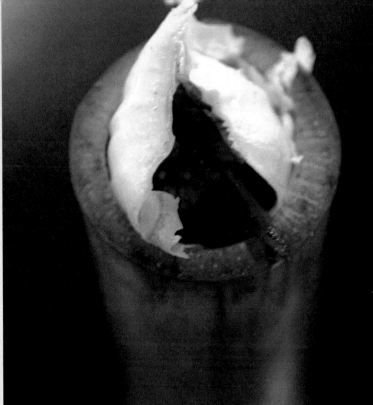

3   Carefully pour chicken stock into the bamboo. With the grill surface at an angle, place the bamboo on the grill with the open side of the bamboo stalk slightly raised above the closed end.

4   Grill on a low heat and rotate often to allow for an even cook. As you rotate the bamboo on the grill, it will become blackened on the outside. *If the bamboo catches fire, extinguish it* to avoid overcooking. Cook for roughly 20-30 minutes or until the fish is thoroughly cooked within the bamboo.

Cooking sticky rice

Boil water in a medium pot. Strain the sticky rice and pour it in the steaming tray above the water pot. Cook until the rice is raised and softened.

Chili sauce

Crush Thai chili, 2 cloves of garlic, and sugar together in a mortar and pestle. Add fish sauce and lime juice and stir together with a spoon. Remove and place the sauce in small sauce ramekin.

Enjoy

Remove the fish from the bamboo and remove the lemongrass stalk. Eat the fish with the chili sauce and sticky rice.

Blue Cheese and Spinach Stuffed Pork Loin

Matt Wells

In an attempt to capture a float experience I made a stuffed pork chop. I tried to make each ingredient remind me of floating in a dark room with no light or sound.

Obviously there is no light or sound inside a pork chop, so I started there. Spinach and blue cheese work to represent the smooth and salty feeling you get while melting away as you float in your small water cave. The rub was a little more difficult. Cayenne pepper and garlic represents the stinging, itchy feeling I got in the small scratches on my skin I was unaware of until I got into the salty abyss. For the sauce, I just put everything together: bourbon for the relaxation, cream and cheese to make it a thick, slow-moving sauce that reminds me of slowly dragging myself out of my floating oasis and back to reality.

Having never floated before, I was unsure at first on how to explain my experience in a dish. Open to the challenge, this is what I made. Upon my second float, I realized that it was probably impossible to fully get my experience across and have another person relate.

Everyone floats differently, right? Having plenty of time to do so in a dark watery room, I broke down my float piece by piece and put it back together, thinking of the parts of my float that stuck out in my head.

Matt Wells is a chef at the Brooklyn House Restaurant – brooklynhouserestaurant.com

Ingredients

Recipe serves one person

12-20 inches of butcher string

Filling

7 ounce pork loin chop

½ ounce of spinach

½ ounce of blue cheese

Pork rub

½ teaspoon of cayenne pepper

1 tablespoon of sea salt

1 tablespoon of pepper

Sauce

½ ounce of blue cheese

1 ounce of bourbon

⅛ cup of cream

¼ cup of beef or chicken stock

½ tablespoon of coarse sea salt

Directions

1 Start by cutting the pork loin almost in half through the side, leaving the two sides partially attached.

2 Mix the spinach and blue cheese together in a separate bowl.

3 Fill the pork chop with spinach and cheese mixture.

4 Using butcher string, tie the two halves closed to keep the filling inside.

5 Rub entire outside of the pork chop with pork rub ingredients above.

6 Place sauté pan on high heat and add oil. Once the oil just starts to smoke, place pork chop in pan facing away from you (the oil will pop).

7 Sear for 1 to 2 minutes until the side facing down is golden brown.

8 Flip pork chop and place in 500° F oven for 8 to 10 minutes or until internal temperature is 155° F. Remove pan from oven. Remove pork chop from pan and set aside.

9 Put the same pan back on high heat and deglaze with bourbon. Be careful, as depending on your stove, some flames may result.

10 Add stock, cream, and cheese. Let reduce until the edges of the sauce start to brown and remove from heat.

11 Garnish with coarse sea salt. Goes great with roasted red potatoes or seasonal vegetables.

Desserts & Drinks

Desserts

Floating Piegasm ⑥ⓥ — 64

Poppy Panna Cotta — 66

Roasted Strawberry Rhubarb Crisp ⓥ — 70

Vegan Chocolate Coconut Tart ⓥ — 74

Bites from the Void ⑥ⓥ — 78

Refreshing Sorbet ⑥ⓥ — 82

Drinks

Summer Shirt ⑥ⓥ — 86

Mourning Becomes Her ⑥ⓥ — 88

Berry Tonic ⑥ⓥ — 90

Floating Piegasm

Angella Davis

Upon completing my first float, I was hungrier than I have ever been, but fully committed to only putting healthy food into my body.

From this, a Floating Piegasm was created. A piegasm is the all over body high you get when you eat something that is entirely good for you.

Ingredients

Recipe serves six to eight people

3 figs

3 dates

2 tablespoons of almonds
finely ground

2 tablespoons of hazelnuts
finely ground

3 bananas

**1 tablespoon of cashews
or macadamia nuts**

1 teaspoon of pumpkin pie spice

4 strawberries *sliced*

a small handful of blueberries

a small handful of raspberries

1 pinch of coconut flakes

Tools

1 eight inch pie plate

food processor

Directions

1 Use a food processor to make a paste of the figs and dates.

2 In the bottom of a small pie pan, press hazelnuts and almonds alternatively with the date-fig paste. Press down starting in the middle and work your way outwards.

3   Slice the bananas into the pie pan.

4   Sprinkle the cashews or macadamia nuts on top of the bananas.

5   Sprinkle the pumpkin pie spice on top of the cashew or macadamia nuts.

6   Arrange the strawberries, blueberries, and raspberries on top of the banana filling.

7   Sprinkle the coconut flakes on top

8   Eat. *Repeat often!*

Poppy Panna Cotta

Sophia LeBlanc

In my relaxed state within the salt bath, I was taking all my senses in, even when they felt somewhat dreamy.

With my dessert, I incorporated the rosy color of my skin and thought about juicy strawberries. The panna cotta reminded me of the lotion and the smooth texture of the way my skin felt. The almond cookie reminded me of the textured wall of the float tank, and the poppy seeds of the grainy texture of the salt.

I tried to evoke — in this dessert — the way I felt lying there in the salt bath.

Floating in the tank evoked the foundation of the almond cookie, the strawberries appear as the juices of the bath, the panna cotta related to my milky skin and the poppy seed represented the grainy texture of the salt. It was a wonderful space to be in, with many contrasting layers and in a dreamy, relaxed state.

Sophia LeBlanc is a chef and instructor based out of Portland. For catering or upcoming classes visit – worldeats.org

Ingredients

Recipe serves four people

Panna Cotta

1½ cups of heavy whipping cream

½ cup of 2% milk

¼ cup of sugar

2½ sheets of gelatin

1 teaspoon of poppy seeds

1 tablespoon of lemon zest

Poppy Seed Shortbread Cookie

8 ounces of unsalted butter

4 ounces of sugar

a pinch of salt

1 egg

1 tablespoon of vanilla

12 ounces of all purpose flour

1 tablespoon of poppy seeds

½ cup of sliced almonds

Directions

Panna Cotta

1   In ice-cold water, place gelatin sheets until they soften. Drain excess liquid.

2   Bring heavy cream, milk, and sugar to a boil.

3   Whisk in softened gelatin sheets until dissolved.

4   Add poppy seeds and 1 tablespoon of lemon zest.

5   Let mixture cool to room temperature before placing in serving vessels. Chill in refrigerator to set up "cooked cream" for a few hours, or ideally overnight.

6   Serve in round shape plexi-molds, or wine glasses.

Poppy Seed Shortbread Cookie

Serve Poppy Seed Panna Cotta with Poppy Shortbread Cookie

1   With a paddle attachment in a mixer on low speed, cream the butter, sugar, and salt until very soft.

2   Add the egg and the vanilla.

3   Add the flour but do not mix all the way.

4   Add the almonds and poppy seeds. Mix dough until just combined.

5   Shape cookies to about 2 ounce disks.
Flatten out dough to desired shape.
Bake at 325° F for approximately 10 to 12 minutes. Let cool.

Strawberry Garnish

1   For each serving, add Strawberry Garnish to the Poppy Panna Cotta. Start by using ½ cup of sliced strawberries, sweetened to taste with granulated sugar.

2   Mix and sprinkle with 1 teaspoon of lemon zest.

Roasted Strawberry Rhubarb Crisp
with Brown Butter Oat Crumble

Katie Shyne

Lying in the womb-like dark of a float tank made me think of beginnings. The moment when something is born. My first memories revolve around my mother's garden and the beginning of spring.

The first thing I ever learned to bake was a rhubarb crisp. I decided to revisit the family recipe I learned as a child and make it better, worthy of the lifelong memories it elicits.

All the steps in this recipe can be prepared in advance if desired.

Ingredients

Recipe serves four to six people

1 cup of brown sugar

1 cup of pastry flour

1 cup of rolled oats

1 cup of butter *browned*

1 teaspoon of cinnamon

1 teaspoon of salt

2 cup of hulled strawberries

¼ cup of sugar

1 lime

4 cup of rhubarb

½ cup of sugar

1 inch piece of fresh ginger *grated*

¼ cup of flour

½ cup of freeze-dried strawberries *ground in a spice grinder*

½ cup of sugar

Directions

1. Preheat oven to 375° F.

2. Toss the brown sugar, pastry flour, rolled oats, butter, cinnamon, and salt together until moist, spread evenly on a cookie sheet, bake for 15 minutes and set aside.

3. Place the strawberries, ¼ cup of white sugar, and lime juice in a deep baking dish. Cover with foil and bake for 10 minutes or until the berries start to release their juices. Repeat that process with a ½ cup of white sugar, rhubarb, and grated ginger. The rhubarb will take longer, approximately 20 minutes. Strain as much of the cooking liquids from the strawberries and rhubarb into a small pot and add the remaining ingredients. Whisk on the stovetop at medium heat until bubbling and thick.

4. Mix all of the cooked wet ingredients together. Place in the bottom of a deep baking dish and sprinkle the brown butter crumble from step 2 on top. Place back into the oven until the filling is bubbling up through the topping.

Serve with ice cream or whipped cream

Vegan Chocolate Coconut Tart

Sean McGlohon & Samantha Ellis

Slipping into a meditation, like floating on a cloud, allows one to leave the body behind.

As a yoga instructor, I dance between this space to find balance, stillness, and awareness.

I wanted to create a dish that tasted like a lucid dream. Chocolate was a desired ingredient because research suggests that it helps to activate serotonin neurotransmitters, while the smoothness of coconut lifts my spirits towards the sky.

Ingredients

Recipe serves six people

Crust

½ cup of margarine or Earth Balance *softened*

⅓ cup of vegan sugar

¾ cup of finely chopped cashews

1 teaspoon of vanilla

1½ cups of all purpose flour

Filling

10 ounces of bittersweet chocolate *coarsely chopped*

1½ cups of unsweetened coconut milk *or other dairy substitute*

1 tablespoon of tapioca starch *arrowroot starch or corn starch can be used as substitutes*

2 tablespoon of coconut oil

1 teaspoon of vanilla extract

Coconut Shavings *roasted Hazelnuts, berries, etc. for topping*

Directions

1 Preheat oven to 350° F.

2 In a large bowl, cream together margarine and sugar with a whisk, until smooth.

3 Stir in cashews and 1 teaspoon of vanilla.

4 Add flour, a little at a time, until combined, but slightly moist.

5 Press into 9 inch pie dish, and place in oven for 15-20 minutes, or until lightly browned.

6 Remove from oven and set aside to cool.

7 Meanwhile, place chopped chocolate into a large bowl. In a medium saucepan, whisk together coconut milk with tapioca starch until combined.

8 Bring to a light boil over medium-high heat, and remove from stovetop. Whisk in coconut oil and pour over chocolate, stirring to melt the chocolate.

9 Add 1 teaspoon of vanilla extract and mix well until smooth.

10 Pour chocolate mixture over the prepared crust.

11 Cover pie and place in the refrigerator for a minimum of four hours to cool.

12 Once chilled and firm, the pie can be garnished with coconut shavings, nuts, berries, or any toppings of choice for desired taste and texture.

Bites from the Void

Alexandra Upton

When beginning this project, I knew I wanted to create something that was tantalizing to the imagination as well as the senses while still providing nutritional value.

I wanted to enter the abyss with just these intentions and a blank slate, but alas, the outside world always has an influence embedded in your memories.

During the first float, my brain was consumed with the thoughts of sweet and spicy flavors as a new friend had shared a scrumptious pumpkin-cardamom-spiced raw cookie previously that morning. I wanted to meditate on flavor combinations a little, but I really just wanted to sink into the void and come back with whatever secrets it had to unfold.

Midway through that first float — where thoughts become irrelevant, just feeling — the idea of layers and mixtures of textures ranging from smooth to crunchy came to mind. I set this inspiration aside, to be explored in the kitchen later, still letting go of thought and sinking deeper. Another stroke of inspiration seemed to beam its way across my palette: pumpkin spice with coconut cream all pulled together with cacao.

While shopping for ingredients, another thought hit me: candied ginger to top it off. It's beautiful to the eye and really pulls the spices together from the bottom.

Playing with ingredients, I landed on maple for my sweetener with the help of the dates. In combination with the pecans, you get a warm buttery sweetness without the dairy or cane sugar.

The first test run produced a bar-shaped dessert consisting of all the ingredients and a similar process, but I found this difficult to serve and consume.

After float number three, I decided to turn the bars into bite-sized, bonbon-style treats.

I hope your enjoyment of these treats equals the joy I get when I witness others experiencing them.

To create these treats, you will need a high-powered blender and a food processor.

Ingredients   *Recipe makes 16 to 20 bite-sized servings*

Filling

1 cup cashews, soaked 2-4 hours

1 cup shredded coconut

¼ cup maple syrup

1 vanilla bean *scraped*

½ cup of filtered water
extra ½ cup on the side

Frosting

½ cup maple syrup

¼ cup coconut oil

⅔ cup raw cacao

Additional

½ cup crystallized ginger *crumbled*

Crust

Wet ingredients

½ cup pitted medjool dates
soaked 15 to 30 minutes

½ cup of pumpkin

½ cup of maple syrup

1 tablespoon of melted coconut oil

1 tablespoon of lemon juice

Dry ingredients

1½ cups of almond flour

¾ cup of oat flour

1½ teaspoons of cinnamon

½ teaspoon of cardamom

½ teaspoon of nutmeg

½ teaspoon of clove

½ teaspoon of fresh ginger

½ teaspoon of Himalayan pink salt

½ cup of pecan

¼ cup of coconut palm sugar

4 to 5 pitted medjool dates

Directions

Crust

1 Combine all wet ingredients in a high-powered blender. Blend until relatively smooth. If the mixture is too thick, add a tablespoon of water and blend again. If necessary, add more water, a tablespoon at a time until you achieve a smooth consistency.

2 Combine almond flour, oat flour, cinnamon, cardamom, nutmeg, clove, ginger, and pink salt in a large bowl and set aside.

3 Combine pecans and palm sugar in a food processor and pulse until coarsely ground. Add dates one or two at a time and pulse to incorporate until mixture becomes crumbly. Place in large bowl.

4 Add wet ingredients and pecan-date crumble to dry ingredients. Thoroughly mix, using your hands, a wooden spoon, or a sturdy spatula. Place in fridge and let firm for at least 2 hours.

Filling

1 Place all ingredients in a high-powered blender and process until smooth. If too thick, add 1 tablespoon of water at a time as in Step 1 for the crust.

2 Transfer to a bowl and place in fridge. Let mixture firm for at least 2 hours.

Frosting

Add maple syrup to blender first, followed by coconut oil and cacao powder.

Assembly

1 Using about a tablespoon of the crust mixture at a time, form into balls. With your thumb, make a cup-like indentation in each ball.

2 Fill indentation with about a tablespoon of filling.

3 Cover with frosting as desired and top with ginger pieces.

4 Place in freezer for at least 4 hours.

Enjoy!

Refreshing Sorbet

Erica Stephensen

After floating in salt water, I really feel like I just need to rehydrate. Cucumbers and watermelon are what I crave in the summer time — they're both so light and refreshing. Coconut water is also full of electrolytes, which is an added bonus.

Of course, you can always just fill up a big bowl and savor the sorbet on its own... but I like to bring out the coconut by introducing the crisps and whip cream. This sorbet is the perfect thing to enjoy after a deliciously relaxing float. I hope you'll agree.

Ingredients

Recipe makes about 1 quart
Serves one to six people

¾ to 1 cup of watermelon juice

⅓ cup of cucumber juice

½ cup of coconut water

1 can of coconut milk

½ cup of agave

½ cup of unrefined evaporated cane juice

1 lime for lime juice
about ⅛ of a cup

Directions

1   Juice the watermelon, then the cucumber. You won't need a whole one of either. Drink the rest or make a bigger batch of sorbet!

2   Crack open the coconut using the back of a chef's knife. If it's your first time, make sure that you remember to break it over a bowl. Measure out the coconut water needed and enjoy the rest. You can use packaged coconut water, but it's definitely not as good. Stay away from the canned kind — it has a funky metallic taste.

3   Add sweeteners and whisk until combined.

Directions continued...

Directions

4   Balance with lime juice. You may need 2-3 limes depending on your taste and that of the watermelon. I would not recommend reducing the sugar however.*

5   Churn according to your ice cream machine's instructions.**

6   You can transfer it into a container, cover the surface with plastic wrap, and freeze the rest. (I prefer to eat it immediately. The texture is so smooth and delicious!)

7   It will freeze pretty hard due to its low sugar content.*

8   The next time you want to enjoy it, pull it out of the freezer for a few minutes to soften a little, and scrape it with the side of a metal spoon.

9   Scoop above mixture into a shallow dish and freeze until partially set.

10 Scrape with a fork and put it back in the freezer for about 20 minutes.

11 Repeat 2-3 times until frozen into coarse crystals similar to a snow cone.

12 Place scoops of Sorbet on a bowl or plate garnished with Coconut Crisps and Coconut Whipped Cream.

Sugar directly affects the freezing point. Adding a little bit of vodka or other liquor will lower the freezing temperature and make it set softer. Be careful though... too much booze and it'll always be slushy. You decide if that's a warning or a suggestion.

**If you do not have an ice cream machine or just prefer the texture, follow a procedure for making granita...*

Coconut Crisps

1   ½ cup of agave

2   ¼ cup of coconut *unsweetened, fine*

3   Add a pinch of quality sea salt

4   Prepare a cookie sheet with baking parchment or a silpat if you've got one.

5   Squeeze or spoon agave onto sheet in long ovals. Give them some room... They will spread a lot.

6   Sprinkle each with a good amount of coconut.

7   Sprinkle very lightly with sea salt.

8   Bake at 375° F until golden.

9   Place as desired.

10 Serve immediately.

Coconut Whipped Cream

1   Freeze can of coconut milk to separate cream.

2   Thaw and remove separated cream layer.

3   Infuse with 3-5 fresh basil leaves *optional*

4   Remove leaves before whipping.

5   Sweeten if you wish. I don't find it necessary when paired with the watermelon.

Summer Shirt

Kimberly Malone

When I was in the tank I kept opening and closing my eyes, attempting to see some sort of difference. Why do eyelids closed feel so inward moving? Suddenly there was light — a real sense of light and light-bright white filled my conscious space. My heart smiled, considered this for a moment, when a rest, deep rest came on. Sudden spring time. Poof, poof, pompoms everywhere. Pink ruffles, white papers green slivers. Sun spots.

Kaboom.

Tools

Pint Glass

Muddler

Shaker

Strainer

Glassware

Cocktail Glass

Directions

1 In your pint glass, combine your lemon juice, lemon balm, and St. Germain.

2 Add a few cubes of ice and muddle the contents of the glass for 45 seconds or so.

3 Add more ice to fill pint glass.

4 Add aquavit and bitters.

5 Place shaker on top of pint and shake until metal is almost too cold to hold comfortably.

6 Strain contents into cocktail glass.

7 Garnish with a bud of lemon balm.

Kaboom!

Ingredients

¼ ounce of fresh lemon juice

3 tablespoons of fresh lemon balm
just estimate

½ ounce of St. Germain

1½ ounce of Krogstad Aquavit

dash of plum bitters

Mourning Becomes Her

Kimberly Malone

From the deep rest I was aroused by images of putrid flesh — grotesque horrors of decay and rot. Somehow the scent was healthy, dank and green dark. Beautiful was the final gift.

Tools

Pot or Kettle

Glassware

A clear glass mug *or any beautiful tea cup that can comfortably hold 10 ounces*

Directions

1   Add tea flower to your glassware.

2   Add boiling water and allow it to steep for 5 minutes.

3   Add Cointreau, Cherry Heering, and Rum.

4   Garnish with lemon twists.

Enjoy!

Ingredients

1 Black Peony Tea Flower
Tao of Tea (brand)

6 ounces of boiling water

½ ounce of Cointreau

½ ounce of Cherry Heering liqueur

1½ ounces of Limited Release rum
House Spirits Distillery (brand)

2 lemon twists

Berry Tonic

Sean McGlohon & Samantha Ellis

After being immersed in water for an extended period of time, I found myself having an unquenchable thirst. It seemed as if I could drink glass after glass of water and still not be satisfied. Having studied nutrition, I learned that a rainbow of colors should be in every meal to provide a plethora of nutrients. Combining this desire for hydration and nutrition I decided to add some fresh seasonal berries. Who knew a glass of water could be so tasty!

Tools

Muddler

Glassware

Clear pint glass or mug

Directions

1 Add fruit to the bottom of a pint glass, and then muddle the fruit until crushed.

2 Add water and stir together well until flavors mix.

3 Separate crushed fruit from the remaining liquid. Add slices of cucumber to the glass with liquid. Add a few cubes of ice or chill until ready to serve.

Enjoy!

Ingredients

2 cups of water

10 blueberries

2 raspberries

3 thin slices of cucumber

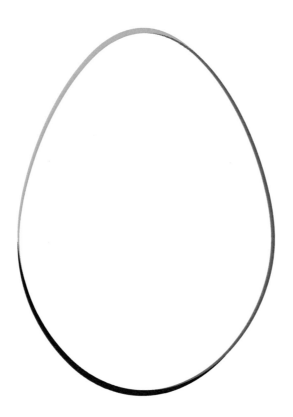

Chefs

Charles Grey O'Neill

Robert "Bama" Pugh

Jeffrey MacKay

Kerri Sullivan

Samantha Ellis & Sean McGlohon

Izzeldin Bukhari

Linda Dalal Sawaya

Rob Walls

Jake Farrar

Matt Kedzie

Sarah Arkwright

Carrie Woods

Daisy Bactad

Tanasapamon Rohman "Goy"

Matt Wells

Angella Davis

Sophia LeBlanc

Katie Shyne

Alexandra Upton

Erica Stephensen

Kimberly Malone

Photography by

John Petty

Jessica Foster

Samantha Ellis

Sean McGlohon

Garrett Kemp-Lowe

Mike Hisashi Rohman

European-Style Comfort Food

3131 SE 12th Ave, Portland, OR 97202

Our hosts at The Brooklyn House Restaurant opened up their kitchen and restaurant which made it possible to prepare, photograph, and taste a number the recipes found in this book.

The Brooklyn House Restaurant staff is committed to offering delicious European-style comfort food that is consciously sourced, healthfully prepared and affordably priced. We source all of our meats directly from very small Oregon farmers, as well as our eggs. We source our fresh pasta, bread, coffee, tea and sparkling mineral water from local, Portland based companies. Our beverage list offers a wide range of small-batch craft wines, beers, ciders, spirits and non-alcoholic drinks. The desserts are freshly prepared from scratch with the finest ingredients available, including locally roasted cocoa and locally harvested fruits and oats.

Over time, our direction has come into focus as a nutritionally based restaurant. Naturopathic doctors all over the city have started recommending us to their patients because of our empathic staff and wholesome food. Most of our guests are mindful of their own unique relationship with food, and we have learned that "healthy" is different for everyone. Often folks feel bashful about verbalizing an entire list of food allergies and personal preferences, so we encourage our guests to open up and share those lists. We sincerely applaud people who have chosen to take control of their own nutritional health and we want to know how we can provide a delicious meal without compromises. Working with whole, fresh ingredients makes this whole process a breeze for us.

brooklynhouserestaurant.com

1235 SE Division St, Portland, OR 97202

Double Dragon was the second site for a making and tasting session. Here is a little about the hospitality you will find at this local Portland, Oregon eatery:

Double Dragon is a bar that also happens to serve **banh mi voted #1 in town** by *the Portland Mercury.*

We've got a solid list of classic, affordably priced cocktails as well as some signature cocktails of which we're very proud. A rotating cast of microbrews are poured on four taps along with a strong selection of canned and bottled beers. Happy hours run weekdays 3pm-6pm and feature compelling deals like $10 for a pint of draft beer and one of our very filling and fairly slept-on burgers.

We prepare these and all of our food using local, sustainable ingredients whenever possible. In all cases, we use only natural, hormone and antibiotic-free meat and eggs. We host live music from time to time and we're extremely proud to host Baby Ketten Karaoke every Saturday night from 9pm-2am.

Our staff is super friendly and when we're not working, we're most likely doing "research" at one of any number of the other awesome bars in this crazy, lovely city. Come see us!

doubledragonpdx.com

Float Tanks

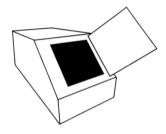

Let's start with the basics: a float tank is essentially the perfect bath tub. They vary in size, but the typical tank is 8' long and 4' wide. Air is allowed to freely flow in and out, and the door never locks or latches.

It holds about 10" of water, which is saturated with 850 pounds of Epsom salt. This creates a solution more buoyant than the Dead Sea, and you float on your back about half in and half out of the water.

The water itself is kept at the average skin temperature (93.5° F), which allows you to lose track of your body. The tank is sound proof and, when you turn off the light, completely dark.

No gravity, no touch, no sound, and no sight. Let's explore what all this does.

The buoyancy puts your body into what is essentially a zero-gravity environment: your muscles and bones get to relax, your joints and spine decompress, and the strain on your circulatory system is greatly reduced. The energy that your body usually spends fighting old man gravity is suddenly available for healing and rejuvenation. It's basically like your entire body breathing a sigh of relief.

view from inside a float tank

Once you're in this state of relaxation, your brain waves lower their frequency from our waking alpha and beta states down into a theta state. This is where you go when you daydream, or when you're just drifting off to sleep. Theta waves are typically rooted in the right-hemisphere of your brain and are known for encouraging creativity and inspiration.

With no external stimuli coming in, your system stops worrying about all the background tasks that usually keep it occupied—mostly related to not dying. Your fight-or-flight response gets a chance to kick back and stop bossing your brain around, lowering your production of adrenaline and cortisol. Instead, studies show signs that your dopamine and endorphin levels rise, giving you a natural mood high which often lasts for days.

Sensory deprivation affects us in another notable way; as our brains become stimuli starved, their reaction is to start creating their own stimuli. Swirling nebulas, gorillas on surfboards, and frolicking Labradors are only a sampling of the visualizations that people have reported from their time in the tank.

Artists are moved to put paint to canvas, musicians to put fingers to strings, and chefs—well, you can taste their creations for yourself.

Manufactured in the United States of America.
Design & Composition by Ashkahn Jahromi, Antonio Matic, Graham Talley, Minae Lee, and Josh Fitz in Portland, OR.

Coincidence Control Publishing
4530 SE Hawthorne Blvd
Portland, OR 97215
coincidencebooks.com
(503) 384-2620

The serif typeface used in this book is Aldus, designed by Hermann Zapf in 1954—the same year as the first float tank.

The sans-serif typeface is Avenir, designed by Adrian Frutiger in 1988—the font was chosen for its effective combination of: Book, *Book Oblique*, Light, *Light Oblique*, and **Heavy** weights.

Ordering Information:
Special discounts are available on quantity purchases.
Contact Coincidence Control Publishing for more information.

23188735R00065

Made in the USA
San Bernardino, CA
08 August 2015